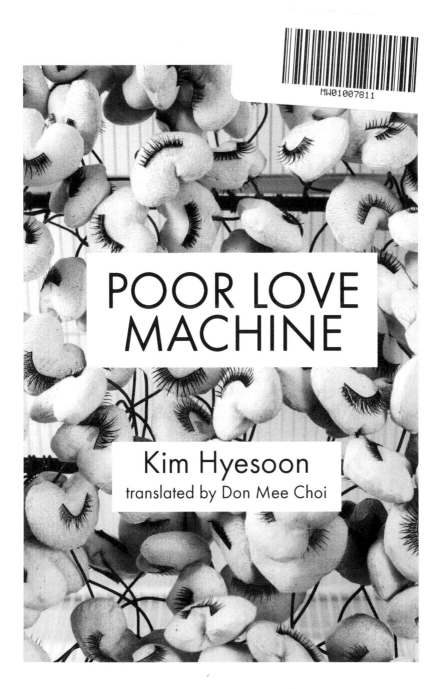

POOR LOVE MACHINE

Kim Hyesoon
translated by Don Mee Choi

ACTIONBOOKS

Notre Dame, Indiana 2016

Action Books

Joyelle McSweeney and Johannes Göransson, Editors

Nichole Riggs, Assistant Editor, 2014-2016

Chris Muravez and Zachary Anderson, Assistant Editors, 2015-2017

Andrew Shuta, Book Design

ISBN 9780900575754

Library of Congress Control Number: 2016933050

Poor Love Machine is published under the support of Literature Translation Institute of Korea (LTI Korea).

 LTI Korea
Literature Translation Institute of Korea

Cover image 'A Hencoop at Midnight' ©2014 by Fi Jae Lee; fijaelee.com

Write to us at:

356 O'Shaughnessy Hall, Notre Dame, IN 46556 or visit us online at actionbooks.org.

"Kim Hyesoon is Korea's most important living poet and by far its most imaginative writer... she and Don Mee Choi have become the most important writer-translator partnership in Korea in the new millennium." Bruce Fulton, Young-Bin Min Chair in Korean Literature and Literary Translation, University of British Columbia

"...she creates a seething, imaginative under-and over-world where myth and politics, the everyday and the fabulous, bleed into each other. Her enormously energetic poems are full of dizzying transitions and tonal shifts." Sean O'Brien, *Independent*

"Kim Hyesoon portrays a panorama of hovering love-hate feelings for the birthing body and for the cruelty of existence, creating an expansively conceived and dizzyingly borderless cosmic geography." Aase Berg

"I first heard Kim Hyesoon at Poetry Parnassus, the global festival of poetry which took place in London's Olympic year. Kim Hyesoon shared the stage with Seamus Heaney. It was the last time I heard Seamus Heaney read in public and the first time I heard Kim Hyesoon, and even at the time it felt momentous.... The birdlike Kim Hyesoon wove a pattern of poems, so strangely compelling and curious, and utterly unlike anything I had heard before." Sasha Dugdale, Editor of *Modern Poetry in Translation*

"Don Mee Choi's dynamic translation brings Hyesoon's miserable, beautiful body into English pungent and fresh, both alive and dead. Her informative introduction provides readers in English the context to interpret these poems as responses to patriarchal, neoliberal, neocolonial control, at once resistance to and inscription of the trauma inflicted by that control." Molly Weigl, translator of *In The Moremarrow* by Oliverio Girondo

"Kim Hyesoon's new book is armament and salve, shield and medicinal chant. It's here to protect us." Christian Hawkey

"... a giddyingly exciting poet and critic." Dougal McNeill, *Overland*

"Her poems are not ironic. They are direct, deliberately grotesque, theatrical, unsettling, excessive, visceral and somatic. This is feminist surrealism loaded with shifting, playful linguistics that both defile and defy traditional roles for women." Pam Brown

"Choi's translations excel, in fact, in how she allows the language to perplex us; she is unafraid of sacrificing the coherence of English grammar if she can maintain a trace of Kim's linguistic play." Mia You, *Bookforum*

"In Kim, the body is inextricably and painfully knitted into the industrial landscape...In this topology, darkness governs. But Kim sides with darkness." Joel Scott, *Cordite*

"Kim's poems, whether lineated or in prose, whether mythic or idiosyncratic (though rarely only one of these for long), reside at precisely those places between what the body is and what it is not, between the corporeal machinery by which meaning is generated and the meanings which thus emerge, tethered to the body by a string of cat guts and vibrating words." Jessica Lawson, *Jacket2*

"From transfigurations of dust mites into microscopic kittens and kitchens into infernos that conjures Ezra Pound's Hell Cantos...the poems within this volume return the reader again and again to the sometimes sublime but often brutal fact that we, like all animals, dwell within transient, vulnerable bodies." Jonathan Stalling, *LIST*

"Kim Hyesoon's fearless poetics suggests a grossly visceral alternative to the capitalist world. These poems conjure both feelings of desire and disgust, awe and repulsion. I want to read more. I need it. Please stop. Don't stop. You make me sick." Christine Shan Shan Hou, *Hyperallergic*

"The limits of creativity here are so wide that very quickly we find we've fallen through the holes old wars blew open, into something like the endless dreams of millions dead." Blake Butler, *Vice*

"While most people seem blinded by Capital, [Kim Hyesoon] shines her spotlight on things that are dark and absurd, the comic and horrifying at the same time." *Swedish Public Television*

"... for Kim Hyesoon, poetry engages directly in a political struggle in which Korean women articulate a "new voice" that allows them to inhabit multiple and fluid identities free of restrictive gender norms..." Ruth Williams, *Guernica*

POOR LOVE MACHINE

Kim Hyesoon

translated by Don Mee Choi

I

II

Rat

Enter the inside of the sunny morning, and it seems as if the scream can always be heard. It's so loud that it's inaudible to us. The scream let out by last night's darkness. This morning the whitish scream suddenly disperses then gathers in the air—*ah, ah, ah, ah*! Do people know how much it hurts the darkness when you turn the light on in the middle of the night? So I can't turn on the light even when the night arrives. The day of the first snowfall, I took an x-ray of my body. Then I asked everyone I met: Have you ever turned on the light inside your intestine? The darkness with a fluid mass moving through it endlessly—is this my essence? When the light is switched on inside my darkness, I buzz like a beetle pinned down, *bzzz, bzzz, bzzz, bzzz*, and shake my head wildly, my mandibles holding onto a black string. Struck by the light, I regress, in a flash, from a reptile to a beetle turned upside down. My dignity is the dark inside. Was it hiding inside the darkness? Lights on—my underground prison, my beloved black being trembles in it. The damaged walls of my room quiver from the car lights coming in through the windows. Thousands of light-rays poke at me—my dark, crouched face. The day of the first snow, the snow was nowhere to be seen. The houses with lit windows. How painful the light must be for the night.

A Teardrop

He picks up a teardrop with a pair of tweezers. My room is lifted up. My face, too, of course. When I calmly sit with my knees raised, it feels as if he is holding in his hands a room where the water flows in through its ears. He places the room under a microscope. An eye bigger than my room looks down at me. I wonder if looking through the lens is like looking into a kaleidoscope. He rolls the room around this way and that. He even blows it about, *huff huff.* Every time his breath touches the room that can so easily burst, it shakes wildly. An eye larger than the house encloses the room. It's as if the blinking sky has drawn near. He uses a stronger lens. A single ray of light enters like a freezing cold sun rising inside the room, the room that is like a wrecked ship. A clutch of eggs is found hidden beneath a wardrobe. Seaweed uncoils. Plankton from the inside of the body that fills up the teardrop is also found. Like a diver, he makes his way through the teardrop. As if a plug has been removed, things swirl inside my head. He whom I called out for in the middle of the night, stirs me about. Unable to endure any longer, the room built with water finally bursts. A teardrop courses down my face and spreads. The wave that shakes my shoulders gnaws away at this entire dark room. At dawn, far away, outside the window, someone as small as a dot walks by, dragging a dog.

Blue Period

Barcelona's Picasso takes flight in the Blue Period before flying off to Paris
The blue powder ground from the meeting of the sky and sea
like two flat stones on top of one another
blows away above my family

When I pull the blanket over me after a day's work
God who has made my bones
by baking the sea for a long time
calls me back out to sea

A lone sea tree mushrooms
The sea tree's leaves are like the curtain of a sea
When I open the curtain and walk in

my blue photos are submerged in that sea of time
my lover is embraced by a face covered in blue moss

I scoop and scoop the blue color, yet it doesn't get scooped out
(as I turn around in bed pulling the blanket up and down)
Can someone please turn off the sea?

The sound of thousands of televisions splashing about
Please turn off the sound
the rustling sound of putting a blue outfit on my lover

(Somewhere inside my bones
there is a wavering sea somewhere
the sea is being played
non-stop)

How did Picasso cross the sea inside the bone
and enter a pistil of the Red Period?
How did he cross the sea inside the bone?

Fallen Angel

1.

When I tear the screen of my body
holograms burst out
and I can go to you
Even if I don't go myself
I am here and can also be there

A says to B, B says to C, C to D, and D to A
I want to run toward you and explode!
B is so miserable that in the end he forgets his suffering
A scene where a 38-caliber revolver points at the people who are eating
Instantly blood splatters all over the empty rice bowls!
The audience with no emergency exits in their bodies
face the movie screen with their eyes wide open

2.

The woman speaks to the man inside the car. You know that C who gives pedestrians
a scare by spraying ketchup on his body and falls down as if he has been shot. It's
fake, but there's something to it. It could be loneliness or something. Why doesn't it
explode?—that kind of thing. You know, the way your body twirls, feeling so burdened.
So the man replies that he already lives his life feeling like that! And so he claims
that his body begins to twirl when he sits in the same spot for even five minutes. The
woman (totally ignores him) goes on to say, You know that C who barges into a store
that's closed in the middle of the night and forces customers to buy things and wash
their hair. C who leaves the lights on in someone else's store and blabs that the store
also has a heart. That's Z, who's talking about his own film. The kind of film that leaves
the lights on in the dark theater and keeps showing other people's things. So the man
replies, Yes, it's like you are sitting inside me, the car (the heart). Then he goes on to say,
C is massaging a pig that has shed its skin, D is crossing her legs on some guy's bed,
and those killer black stockings with holes in them. How thrilling it would be to have
such a sexy woman clean my room daily while I'm out.

3.

All the films speak:
Modern angels are MAFIA
They need to have mafia connections in order to clean out the brightly lit stores
at night.
An Eastern European film speaks again:
Modern angels are well-mannered, wearing black funeral suits
in preparation for our upcoming death.
The film speaks confidently, You mustn't have any feelings in this kind of work!
The angels are kind beings who point rifles at us
Today my daily angels are five crows with pseudonyms
Blue, White, Brown, Orange, Pink
If you punks are going to trash things, bust my tires

(Like when the entire sea quivers uncontrollably
as a drop of water bursts out from the sea
when a single teardrop is about to burst out from a body
thousands of turtles carrying eggs inside their bellies
run out of the sea, making the sand dune black
A raindrop falls onto the car window)

White Horse

What happens if a white horse suddenly enters my room? What if the horse completely fills my room? What if the horse shoves me into its huge eyeball and keeps me in there? A brightly lit train enters the horse and dark people get off. The sun fades and as the door of the deserted house of the dusk opens, a dark woman clutches her torn blouse and runs out as the stars amass around her ankles. Wait a second, then she goes into the empty house and drinks pesticide then runs out and as she runs she tries to vomit out the horse by holding onto a tree, but the horse never leaves once it has entered. She's unable to cry. She can only hiccup, for the horse's mane is making her neck itch. What if the horse never leaves her body? What if the white horse holds onto the tracks engraved inside her body all night long and won't let a single train enter? What do I do? Do I go and ask the woman who is unable to say a single word because the pesticide has destroyed her vocal cords? Here is my room, but I can't enter or leave. The horse stands aimlessly in the room. What do I do?

Fever

The flowering branches fall out of
the flower wallpaper

My bones are etched onto the floor of the room
like a fish fossil

I watch over myself for a long time, I who have already died

The pavements you laid one by one
the roads inside my body explode

a sticky discharge flows
the pavements shoot out of my body

The shadow that walks with its head down gets rolled up
and repeatedly piles up deep inside me

The silver spoon inside that dish bin
is the only thing that remembers the shape of my lips
even my place among the stars has fallen into the bin

A rat skids in and out of the road inside my mouth
No, there's more than one rat

My head that used to rise from the underground passage, drops and drops again,
is repeatedly buried inside the stone floor

Driving in the Downpour

My chest has dried up like a mummy's so that I have no energy to drink sorrow, even the smell of water is unbearable.

While the cars speed over the puddles of water leaving their elongated red tail lights behind them, why am I going over the Andes alone under the blazing sun? Why are the birds flying out from the flaming hat of the western sky? Why is the face of the mummy in the Lima Museum wet even though it's dead?

Even at night my car's windshield wipers place a cold wet towel on my forehead, and yet why am I still going over the Andes where not even a single patch of green can grow because it is too high up here? Why is this mountain range endless even when I keep going over it again and again? Why does the mummy still clasp its dried-up chest with its arms? Why are the mummy's fingers wet like clay being kneaded on the potter's wheel that has momentarily stopped spinning?

Why is the car at a standstill like a toppled water glass as the raindrops on top of its hood quickly bloom then break apart and rise again like a crown made of water? Why did the car stop moving and stand idly at the street corner? Why did the mummy turn its head sideways and keep still in the middle of going over the Andes where the hot snowfall never gets turned off?

Why am I breathing like a lungfish, opening and closing my mouth, why have I lived so long in the same body, am I sighing under my heavy dress, are my eyes open or closed, in a night of a heavy rainfall why does the vast Andes appear in front of me again and again?

Sunstroke

Get submerged
Get submerged in the blazing sun
Get submerged in the rippling blazing sun
Hear something as I get submerged in the rippling blazing sun
Hear something then don't hear then hear again
as I get submerged in the rippling blazing sun
It's like the voice of someone confessing while softly shaking the boiling sand
It's the voice I have wanted to hear for a thousand years
Hear something then don't hear then hear again then don't again
as I get submerged in the rippling blazing sun
Lie down
Lie down on the floor of the blazing sun
Lie down on the cold floor of the blazing sun
It's so hot that the cold floor of the blazing sun sweats
The sweat of the cold floor of the blazing sun is like a knife blade
Among the blade-like drops of sweat from the cold floor of the blazing sun
the tiny blades that are barely visible beat against my ears
The soft sound of knocking, so the eardrums that are about to tear won't tear
The faraway sound of beating comes from faraway, faraway like an echo
Let me in, let me in, let me in
the sound is so faint that it pleads with its needle-like hands

As my eyes open
a flock of crows darts out from my ears
Their beaks poke at my pupils

A Blood-Clot Clock

Inside my heart there is a clock
that tick-tocks nonstop without skipping a single lifetime
There is a clock that
eats blood and shits blood
and its red branches have
spread all over my body
like the winter ivy with bare stems
encircling the cement clock on top of the tower

I have never been able to
get your clock to chime and no one
has disturbed my blood-clot clock
Does such a wretched clock have any thoughts?
Who was it that taught me—
a hundred years is short, yet a day is long?

I once fainted from staring at the sundial
I once threw my body into the sea
holding onto my clock, but I couldn't make it stop
no matter what kind of trauma or love

Since each of our starting times is different
our watches point to different times
In our house the three of us sit in a circle
and silently feed our clocks
None of us has taken off
a clock and put it on the dining table

Ah ah, I tell you that I love you
in your ear with all my strength
as loudly as I can so your clock can hear me
and get your clock to chime

Is it all true—me saying I love you
and you saying you love me
tick-tocking at three in the afternoon?
We have never gone inside our clocks
As the gust of wind blows outside my clock
the red stems of the winter ivy
shake inside me, *whoosh*
and tears collect in my eyes
Can you stop the clock hands for a moment?
Can you hold the handless clock against your breast?
When I bring my ear to your heart
the blood-clot clock runs by itself, *bam bam*
it chimes right on time

Mummy

I age even when I'm dead

My face gets sunburnt even when I'm dead

If I could compare going around the earth to a single lifetime
then I'm in the Sahara Desert at the moment

My lungs' sea has all dried up
The clams burn up

Every time I take a step
thousands of fingers that clasp my wrists
get crushed hot under my feet

The tattered clothes I embrace blow away like powder
Closed eyes fall

The Story in Which I Appear as All the Characters 1

I can set up a school in which I am all the students. The fifty-year-old-me and the sixty-year-old-me hold on to each end of the rope and a ten-year-old-me plays jump rope—that kind of school. For instance, the now-me can teach the me-in-diapers how to say, Mommy Mommy please come see this, and the middle-school-student-me how to use a sanitary napkin correctly. Perhaps the ten-year-old-me could solemnly teach the sixty-year-old-me, Life is... Once again, for example, I can write a story in which I appear as all the characters. I can write a story in which two of me appear together—the nineteen-year-old-me is dumped by a guy and crazily gets hold of some pesticide and the twenty-year-old-me stares at the man who tears down the wall of our house with an axe because I said I didn't love him. How about this story? A story in which my mom prepares a meal for two, the ten-year-old-me and the sixty-year-old-me. The unmarried-me slaps me on the cheek, the now-me sitting in a park, and the seventy-year-old-me comforts the just-got-slapped-me—that kind of story.

I just opened my bag on the bench
in the park after all the lights have gone out
I've left home tonight like a whiney adolescent housemaid
fed up with serving meals three times a day
three hundred sixty-five days a year
But when I opened my bag
the many-me and the just-left-home-me trembling in the cold
met each other

Look over there, my head that came out of
the bag is hovering above the swing!
An embroidered handkerchief is pinned to my chest
I ran away from the temple kindergarten because I was afraid of Buddha's face
No, that's not right, it was several years before that
when I fell into an empty well and was crying and screaming
Look over there, there I am again

above the streetlights, carrying a bag of sweet sticky bread
bought with the coins I stole from Grandfather's safe
The cute-naked-me comes crawling between my knees
in the puddle of water under my feet
Baby, come over here, I'll let you have my yummy milk
The seventy-year-old-me tries to comfort the forty-year-old-me
and the wind blows down the tree-lined street
My white hair comes undone and sweat beads on my forehead
All the grandmothers and daughters that have come out
of my body rise as moon, as stars
The wind blows every leaf on the trees

I sat next to myself all night long to get warm at my fire
I sat next to myself who was suckling
in my mother's arms the longest
I also touched the seventy-year-old-me's grave of breasts
left with just skin
I left home in winter, yet it was very warm beneath the full moon
as if I were holding a brazier that was starting to cool down

The Story in Which I Appear as All the Characters 2

Take off all the verbs, adjectives, adverbs
that have stuck all winter long
then dust off a two-piece dress
and take it to the cleaners
At the Tonghyŏn Cleaners
well-ironed subjects covered in plastic
hang from the ceiling
Even though the memory vanishes
like water that has been gulped down
the song always remains!
After the flock of chicks play *tweet tweet tweet* and leave
a patch of water parsley sprouts
Even without the subject
(the mountain fills up with a flock of yellow-green chicks)
outside of this breathing object

The Story in Which I Appear as All the Characters 3

Every night when I'm about to fall asleep
I embrace a child
the child not yet born
the me before I had a face and a name
I speak quietly not to wake up that child,
I still have the cold I caught last year
I enter the child
The child that hasn't grown a single footprint long since it was born
The blue child
The child that is still not "me"
The child that is not of the yellow race, not the oldest daughter, and moreover not Kim
Hyesoon
The child soars kicking the earth
The child that is still a young star, essentially a blue flame
The child that has not yet opened its eyes in my mother's womb
The child that will stay alive even if I die

Every night when I'm about to fall asleep
an old woman embraces me curled up
She sleeps in the daytime
and stays awake at night and holds me
The repulsive old woman puts death to sleep
between fleshy wrinkles like those of a placenta
holds me all night and looks down
She enters me
Inside her face the earth has already
revived its entire life span
Inside the endlessly stretched grave of breasts
spring summer autumn winter flowed by millions of times
and the mountains orchestrated their own rhythm
The old woman's name and face have decayed
The old woman is so old that she is a child

The old woman will die only after I die
That thing embraces me

We are stacked like three spoons
On top of a pillow
we turn our faces together
The forty-year-old-me in the middle
grinds her teeth saying,
I'm scared I'm scared

Purgatory

After drinking at Chungmun Beach
did I come back and sleep till night?
It's dark whether I open or close my eyes

Where am I?
Like the world inside a mirror
the light is dark and the darkness is bright like velvet
the dark sea outside the window is harder than a silver tray
the sun and the stars are also dark
People here begin life with death
so birth is the end
I lie somewhere in between death and birth
and emit a quick yawn
Where am I?
Purgatory sneaks into my body, opens my eyes
So when I open the eyes inside me
a swirling dark abyss is afloat in the middle of my head
and a volcanic mountain that sucks up darkness
crumbles down near my heart
I stretch out my arms to touch the wall
The wall lies sideways
keeping the mushy intestines
in its black bone cage
The wall has many secrets
like the time pouch that has swallowed
thousands of movements

With all my strength I get up to turn on the light
As the light comes on first in my mouth
the purgatory of dark light and bright darkness
shrinks up inside me
The me who harbors the exterior
looks around the world outside the mirror
Again, where am I?

Mrs. Elephant's Reply

In reply to the letter you sent
I'm sending an elephant
How deep its hatred must be
if an arm comes out
of the forehead between its eyes
and wildly rolls up things
like tree trunks

and grinds with its millstone-like molars
the scary laughs and swallows them
and crushes everything like a tank
and rolls up anything that moves

How deep its despair must be
if the grey pillows that hold up the elephant's head
for days on end receiving its tears
get stuck to the ears and flap about
In reply to the letter you sent
I'm sending an elephant
flapping its two pillows
annoyed by the arrows of rumor
flying in all directions
Every time the elephant's foot lands
words are erased indiscriminately

How long must it wait still holding its breath
till the ivory of immortality suddenly
shoots from its tightly shut lips
Holes are made in the forest of words

Now I'll tear up the letter smeared by teardrops
and open the window to let out the grey
elephant-hard smoke that filled up the room
Ah, but how can I go out into the street with this sharp ivory
hanging from my mouth?

The Poet and the Glamour Girl Go on a Hike

Tonight the poet and the glamour girl decide to go on a hike. The first part of the trail is flat. The poet is used to easy hikes, but the trail gets rockier as she climbs up. She slips, slides. Behind the poet, the glamour girl snorts: Ha you can't even handle such a short climb. The poet gets more out of breath as she climbs up higher. The breathing of the two is wildly out of sync. The poet nags for a rest. The glamour girl is getting too hot, so she briskly takes off the navy blue sky. Then she asks, Are you cold? Are you cold? and bites the poet's frozen ears. This mountain must have no compassion, compassion, says the poet wanting to put down her heart, which is about to burst, but the trail keeps getting steeper, and the glamour girl who is more experienced urges on the poet who is out of breath: Don't put down your heart yet! If we go back down now it's worse than not having had come up at all. The two stop arguing and watch the wrinkled ridge run up, gasping—it must have burst open a spring. The two make nice and drink the spring water. They drink some and spill some. The water spreads. It freezes under their feet till the ground becomes slippery. Now the poet is totally exhausted: Getting to the summit is too much, a mountain can't be swallowed in a single gulp, and the rhythm of my breathing and walking is out of sync, so this can't become a poem. But the glamour girl who has been memorizing all the shapes of the valleys says, Why give up now when the view is so fantastic? then she unties the sun's belt, unrolling it. The sunset gets released at the corner of the sky and the three temples with ThreeThousandBuddhaEnshrinement CommemorationAllNightThreeThousandBowsDevotionalPrayer written on them suddenly float up inside the poet's panting. *Tinkle tinkle*—the sound of the landscape, as the poet embraces the glamour girl and cries her eyes out. The poet is moved, moved and says, We've finally reached the lit temples. Regardless, the glamour girl closes her eyes and relaxes her hands and says, There's still the ThreeThousandBows to do, and bites into the poet's neck.

Vertigo

Why does it take so long for the light to change?
From where I stood at the crosswalk
somebody's gaze hung from the dark window
of the bank's building across the street
I stared at it for a long time, and it turned out to be me
That woman who is tilted to one side is me
A black Hyundai Grandeur passed by
and there was me again stuck to the glossy car
Why does it take so long for the light to change?
The leaves of the gingko trees next to the crosswalk flicker
In sunlight every single leaf is like a crystal mirror
How repulsive, I am shivering, dangling
from the yellow mirror of every leaf
Once again, as I look up, ah the blue mirror!
The sky is slippery
Smells fishy as I bring my lips to it
like somebody's pupil
Someone was staring at me with a blinding light
through a sun-like magnifying glass
placed on top of the pupil
The light changed and my beloved black mirror, my shadow
leads me across the crosswalk
Someone who is crossing at the same time
throws a cigarette butt at the face of my black mirror
Whose fishbowl am I in?
Today I can't open my eyes like someone who has fallen into a maze of mirrors
Whichever way I look it's all me

39.5 Degrees Celsius

An old female pumpkin walks into the sunlight
Someone enters the pumpkin
That someone flattens the insides of the pumpkin with a wooden roller
the yellowish red fibrous rooms extend in all directions
a forklift flickers by between them
The summer afternoon is as intense as the honey-filled pumpkin

There are 127 seeds inside the pumpkin
inside the 127 seeds, there are 127 pumpkins
and inside those pumpkins, 127 seeds
and inside those seeds, there are 127 x 127 x 127 x 127 pumpkins
Did a yellow nuclear pumpkin bomb explode inside my head?
Who'll take down the sticky telephone lines inside my head?

Mr. Kim cuts up the old pumpkin with a scythe
He says he'll feed it to the cows
It's sticky in the sweltering heat like the insides of the pumpkin
People don't exit from the pumpkin
127 x 127 x 127 x 127 freely enter it
but I can't freely enter it
I can't even cut it up for fodder for my cows
The pumpkin bites down on the seeds that are black inside
and stubbornly ripens away

The Poem I Wrote With You 2
—From a letter of May 4, 1994

I look into the fishbowl where I used to live, the bowl that returned to me with
its arms folded when I unfolded mine. How did I end up standing outside it that
day? I looked at it as if I were a live mirror. The bowl that pressed down on me
for a lifetime. In 1999, water flowed from my body. My body looked like someone
who had just pulled a body out from a swimming pool. My body dripped down
outside my clothes. I buried the bowl between my knees and wept. The bowl
became more slippery. It looked like someone else's face. Then your face slipped
out from it and your eyes evaporated, and, in my hands, your skull crumbled into
powder and melted away like dough. I watched the skull on my knees cry like
a cracked fishbowl. A few years after 2029, didn't my heart go up in flames like
a desert at midday? When I woke up in the morning, you cracked the window
of my heart and threw in hot sand. Didn't dried Baby's Breath fall out when
I opened my mouth? Then years later, maybe it was 2048, I carried the bowl,
and, as I crossed a frozen sea, didn't a stallion made of ice stand up beneath the
frozen sea as snow turned to hail inside my blood vessels? Then several decades
later something that made the white tablecloth black, a bundle that stunk of
something rotten, was still gazing into the fishbowl.

A Page of Landscape That Doesn't Get Erased

It was night when sleep ran as usual
inside the brain like a frog looking for water

The childhood home that I thought dead
walked towards me
The mute lined up and walked past between the bands of sunlight in the yard
I tied a rope high up across the big cherry trees
A handstand next to the rope
my skirt was made of light
Someone played a flute
The sound of the flute reached up to the mountaintop
then hovered on top of the highest peak
Stars fell into the invisible sound even though it was daylight
My skirt made of light
swiftly jumped over the black rope seven times
My grandfather dead in the hospital in Seoul
was on his way back home
Aunties lighted fire in the kitchen
frying the dead ghosts
Now it's Mr. Village Head's turn to be fried
The high-pitched sound that made the house ring was still audible
and the sun was soldering the yard white

The frog looking for water jumped outside my sleep
I fumbled about for my glasses out of habit
and looked around the yard of my childhood

Moonrise

The night sky bowed down like a black well
Stars fell into it
falling and falling infinitely
From far over there, the hem of the woman's skirt
was pulled all the way up to the sky well
Even the dark blue edge of the wave's skirt
ran up to the sky gasping gasping
The woman's body soared up into the sky well
falling higher higher
into space

The birds awoke and perched on a dark branch
As one of them let out a scream
the night's crotch ripped and fishy-smelling blood leaked out

The woman's body arched like a bow
and a lump of white, hot, moist flesh
stuck its head out from under the woman's forest
the wave's dark blue skirt covered the woman

The woman pulled the newborn up to her belly
She opened her blouse drenched in sweat and put the fleshy moon
in it then tied her blouse's bows and nursed her baby
The trees of the night by the foot of the forest
finally let out a sigh of relief, trembling

The Photo Taken at Cuzco

We keep our eyes half-closed. A handful of sunlight pushes down on our eyelids. Only the llama on a leash standing beside the Indian woman next to us keeps its eyes wide open, staring into the lens. In the photo only the llama's eyes are dark and big. A stream of darkness gets sucked onto the inner road of the llama's eyes, yet everything outside of the eyes is transparent. Even our clothes become transparent bit by bit, and Professor Kim's purple safari jacket has just stopped turning white. The moment the llama's eyes blink, our feet rise several inches from the ground and the millions of mashed up blue skies beneath our feet mushroom as if the sky and earth have suddenly opened up millions of hinges. At that moment, the roads of darkness born inside me evaporate and vanish. Did the remoteness of height abandon the muddiness of depth? Our mouths open in shock, and, once again, as the llama in the picture raises its eyelashes one by one, an Inca soldier runs all over the Andean mountain top carrying a message "The enemy has invaded," while beneath his feet the winding trails plunge into the llama's deep eyes. We gently half-close our eyes again. The sound of the sky and earth closing the hinges all at once. The dark roads born inside our bodies are endlessly engraved upon our faces. We all adjust our clothes and walk away from the camera as if embarrassed.

Trespassing Prohibited at Mount Halla

A full moon rose inside the faraway cow

The shaman of Cheju Island is climbing a trail up Mount Halla in the rain
—There's a black cloud above the rain, and a full moon above the black cloud,
   right? I figured as much when I saw it from the plane.

A dried pollock is holding pink paper flowers inside the pouch the shaman is
carrying

Ghosts herding sailboats and running up the road kept appearing in front of my
eyes

The shaman's red skirt floated up to the clouds, then eventually disappeared
—You and I do the same work!

The shaman embraced my wet shoulders like a strong man
She called out her younger sibling who died at seven and the baby I'd lost
They went up to the sky, riding the streaks of rain, then plunged back down,
moaning all night long

In my house of memories the glass windows filled with painful landscapes
rattled and broke one by one

The rain-drenched asters fell to the ground
and with all their might
tried to clean up the shattered glass

The shaman reciting a prayer tucked me under the ceremonial blue skirt while I
lay on a boulder

A white tent was beating like a huge drum
till I was out of the forest that no longer prohibited trespassing
I rode into the morning light, on top of a chicken with a broken neck

Moon

I am bouncing a ball by myself
in an empty playground
When the night wind's footsteps
step on the leaves one leaf one leaf
and again one leaf
at a time
the sound of the bouncing ball
echoes *toing toing*
across the empty ground

You who have escaped from me
toing
toing

I throw the ball into the net!

I throw you
high up!

Are you a hollow made from the blow of my breath?

Tonight
I will tie up your face
in space

If I throw the ball up in the air will the wind also throw me?
Every time the wind throws me up in the air
and hits me *toing toing*
it feels as if the skin of my face
with its holes is getting pulled
tight
Oh, then am I also a hollow
made from someone's breath?

In the totally empty night sky
the sound of someone's hand
hitting the taut moon
toing
toing

The Road as a Theme for a Meal 3

It's itchy somewhere far beneath the sea
As if the meal is being prepared for the umpteenth time
a fish is placed on a chopping board on the kitchen table
The knife comes down on its head—my skull is severed
Instantaneously a blackout far beneath the sea
When the roads are extracted from the body on the chopping board
our rooms inside the sea that are like flowery wallpaper beneath a dim lamp
silently crumble
Blood faintly smears the chopping board
The crumbled room is a mere scandal
Put my finger into the mouth and pull out its gills
I want to shove a finger into the silence and make it vomit
Now it's time to scrape off the scales with the blunt edge of the knife
Our roads inside the water that made our ears itch crumble into bits
I run towards me again, inside me
and bang against the door
It feels as if my heart has become a junkyard
It feels as if my inside is aging at high speed
I mishandle the knife—the scales splatter on the kitchen floor
I take out the intestines. Should I skin it too?
I don't think much about it at all and end up slicing the flesh
What do I do now? The fish has shattered into bits

The Museum is Nowhere in Sight

After I dismiss my class I go up to Mount South in autumn
Should I take the cable car? I close my umbrella and use it as a stick to walk up
the trail

The leaves fall, rustling down as a gust of wind blows in and
a whirlwind sweeps me into the museum

This museum must be a museum of portraits
Trapped inside the glass, his face tilts down, laughs and shakes,
turns around for a second

My lover's face unwraps like a bandage
captured quickly with a palette knife, thickly applied paint

Hair on end, hands in pockets, mashed up faces
I go around and look at the endless portraits in the show till my legs ache

Suddenly raindrops fall, and the museum is nowhere in sight
The blood-stained bandage with tattered ends flutters far from my umbrella

The leaves drop one by one, blow away, sweep under my feet
I have come farther than the cable car

The Shocking Crosscurrent of Blue

Swimming pool. It feels as if I'm swimming in tears. Tears stream down my entire body. My body melts every time it soars up in the air. There are times when tears suddenly push their way in from the outside instead of exiting from the inside.

Inside the wind. My body offers itself to the wind every time I soar up in the air. Like the way poplars offer themselves to the wind, perhaps I've been wind all along.

Swimming pool again. His eyes burst. Everyday eyes that gaze at me burst and spill. I adjust my goggles and plunge into the flood of the burst gaze.

Inside the fish tank. They are embracing each other inside the tank. Their cheeks get squashed behind the glass. They're unable to extend their arms. My gaze zeros in, bit by bit, making them narrower. My gaze chokes the fish tank. They can't even open their eyes. Like the way the sheet of glass is pressing them down, the already-dead-me holds up the glass with all the strength of my arms. Look at my eyes that have become as large as the glass.

As a jealous man, I suffer four times over: because I am jealous, because I blame myself for being so, because I fear that my jealousy will wound the other, because I allow myself to be subject to a banality: I suffer from being excluded, from being aggressive, from being crazy, and from being common.
(Roland Barthes, *A Lover's Discourse*, trans. Richard Howard)

Swimming pool again. It must be raining at the bottom of my heart because the fish that lives down there is wriggling. Moving at a full speed, the school of fish outside follows the fish inside me. The car that was speeding spins out on the wet road.

Winter Tree

Where the leaves have fallen off
wind-leaves are dangling

Love you Love you
The trees that have only
a hunchback road
trap a tree inside a tree
shake their bodies
thinking that the fallen leaves
are still dangling from them

*I was truly sad. It was as if my whole body was going to be scattered. I wanted to tie up
my body, for I couldn't bear it being scattered. So everyday my ribs went around and
around in a circle. Anyway, I love you. You are studded all over my body. And this
probably has nothing to do with you.*

I wrote a letter
Even though the wind didn't blow
the bent roads
broke off
from inside my body
to the outside
plop
plop

The Sea Outside the Aquarium

The sea inside me has dried up
There's a distant mirage in the dried-up sea
We ride the waves together naked
The moonlight washes our naked bodies
Our two tails hit the golden sea *plonk plonk*
Shiny birds pop out from our bodies
As always, pilot fish tickle the bottom of our tummies

The inside of the aquarium is a spiral
When a shark cries somewhere far beyond the aquarium, from the South Pacific
Ocean
the shark inside the aquarium meanders down along the spiral
riding on the sound of the cries every minute till it reaches the deep sea room
yet no matter how far it goes the dry sea's life remains
inside the spiral pocket
A shark
comes up again from near where my toes are
How could the very first sea from the beginning of time
have spit out such sad things
Another shark moves down through my stomach
and someone swims towards me
from the distant South Pacific Ocean
even at night, crossing the dark blue sea, pushing the ice away

The Road as a Theme for a Meal 5
—Delicious Poetry

1

—*Pan-fried azalea petal rice cakes*
The child's nose is bleeding. The child was hit by a ball. The ball was thrown far across
the spring sky. Blood drops on the white apron. Blood smears on Grandmother's
cotton skirt.

—*Scorched rice in water*
Even the dirt on top of the wall around our house was tasty.

—*Flour dumpling soup*
Boil it and pour it into a deep bowl?
The Buddhist nuns chant na-ong-hwa-sang as they begin their outing. They pass
under the magnolia tree.
The nuns look like flour dumplings floating in clear broth.

—*Glass noodles stir fried in sesame oil*
Add beef and wood ear mushrooms?
Fox-rain falls on a sunny day.
The sun stir-fries branches gently, the mushroom in the straws under the big pine
tree opens its eyes, the spirals of my thoughts get endlessly untangled like
Grandmother's white hair, the hand holding a pair of chopsticks smacks its lips inside
the distant cloud.

—*Leafy cabbage soup*
Leftover cabbage leaves from making kimchi for the winter, Grandmother braided the
leaves in moonlight, then hung the braids around the neck of a pillar in the backyard.
The night boiled like cows' gruel. Several anchovies floated about.

—*Grandmother, I prepared a tableful of dishes. Please eat to your heart's content the
spring night of this world.*

2

This road can be smashed and eaten as a garnish.
This road can be placed on top of a fire and boiled for two hours till it becomes
tender enough to be eaten.

This painful road can be marinated just right and eaten
with paprika sprinkled on top, even small amount of garlic added to it.

The road needs to be eaten in order for it to keep growing.
Like the dark green grass on Grandmother's grave—she has fallen asleep after
eating all the roads.

Today I carefully unwind the road that I made with my maternal grandmother
and let my salty seasoned teardrops fall.

—*Grandmother, please eat to your heart's content the spring night of this world.*

Na-ong-hwa-sang was a renowned Buddhist monk in the 14th century of the Koryo period.

Bright Rags

I want to lie down beneath the crotches of the women carrying water jars on
their heads
I want to lie down beneath the crotches of the women climbing up the hill
their water jars filled from the well down below

I want to lie down beneath the tree that harbors the women
and touch their crotches
the women who scoop up the fresh nutrients from the soil and
pour the milk-water into the thick branches and tiny stems
Oof, the fishy smell of the mashed green

The water jars reach the steep stairs
till they can't go any further
and at the tip of the stem
water is poured out onto the precarious sprig
Pink flowers bloom all at once in empty space

A pink flowering tree cleans the empty space
The space that was vacant all winter long is thoroughly wiped for several
afternoons
The huge pink rags held up by the women are bright

Regarding My You

The road gets pulled up
like when my grandmother sits at her loom
and holds the shuttle high
The tense roads of the Lufthansa 718 passengers
who live scattered all over the Earth are pulled tight
328 roads take off

My lover is out of breath
Every kind of leaf is stuck to his nose and mouth
so that he gasps in and out
He still has more to say
Outside the window of the plane a cloud shadow forms
The trees lean to one side
Like the clouds flocking together he opens and closes his mouth silently

The lowest of the low down below
The frightened mountains with green shrunken hair
The rivers dribble saliva on my lover's face, the hardened oceans
Where is my heart tied up?
At what point did my lover soar
then swoop down on me?
The lowest of the low down below
Where did the snow flurries swirl about then wrap his face with a bandage?

Ah, but what am I to do?
The mountains and seas inside your face
with no exit
The more I float and float up
your flat face
that has no height or depth
Grandmother sitting at her loom
holds the shuttle high and says,

Let's hang the Lufthansa 718 in the West
Again, my lover takes me into his embrace

The woven cloth lengthens
When will it release me?
I leave, dragging my suitcase over your face

This Night

A rat
devours a sleeping white rabbit
Dark blood spills from the rabbit cage
A rat devours a piglet that has fallen into a pot of porridge
(chunks of freshly grilled flesh inside a womb,
babies that shiver from their first contact with air,
fattened chunks of flesh,
tasty, warm chunks that bleed when ripped into)
A rat devours the newborn in the cradle
Mommy has gone to the restaurant to wash dishes
A rat slips in and out of a freshly buried corpse

A rat that has never eaten anything that hasn't been stolen,
a rat that molds our shadows into a ball and blows into it to open our eyes,
a rat that silently burrows beneath the fungus between toes,
a rat that curls up its tail while eating voraciously even when it hears the rustle of a
breath,
a rat that secretly watches us couple from behind a hidden camera,
a rat that has to grind its teeth daily, for they continue to grow,
that boasts it has seen entire eons of evolution

In between the tiny blood vessels inside our glaring exterior,
inside the dark slippery intestines beneath the soft skin,
in between the wiggling toes under the creaking floor,
inside the skull where the echoing footsteps of rain and wind hide out,
inside that dark place of my body that not even a single ray of light can penetrate,
inside that belly of the body of death tucked inside my body for years,
a rat grinds its teeth to devour my fingers

this night

The Road as a Theme for a Meal 4

The road continues
then suddenly stops
and opens
green delicate leaves
I weed the road
and boil up soup with it
The road comes over
then suddenly stops
and releases silver pomfrets
into the green seawater
With a knife
I cut out a slice of ocean

Perhaps I mishandled the knife
A slice of road
falls onto my heart
boils like a bright azalea field
I spoon out
the bloody foam of the flowering field

The moon kicks up its heels
soaring
above the crimson bloody road
The road the moon
travels on is fishy

Heavenly Ramen

Like when the sky boils a star for a long time
60 million humans, countless mushrooms
and even more countless fish come out
when you boil the earth's night, the night's delusions
for a long time
(I lift the lid and
watch my boiling brain)

The employee of Nongshim Ramen of Kyŏngi Province, Ansŏng City,
Taedŏk District, Sohyŏn Village, who's explaining that there are plenty of
clams, beef, and vegetables in the soup
sounds as if he is talking about the stars
If you boil the delusions for a long time
new stars burst out
(I rip open the soup pouch
The boiled-then-freeze-dried stars
fall out into the sink)

The hot night is boiling like the pot of ramen
The shoeshine men are having ramen
leaving old shoes strewn on the street
in front of a department store
The stars travelling to the ramen pot
plunge in, Ah it's hot, ah it's hot

And this single bowl of ramen
each sky that you and I boil with reverence
but ultimately cannot be crossed…
(As soon as I turn off the stove my bloated brain
melts into the reddish broth)

A Stuffy Poet and a Precocious Lover

The moment the poet says that the museum's narrative is chronological, his lover says that the museum can be read backwards and even starting from the middle as she pushes her shoes between his ribs. As soon as the poet says: Reading in that way is impossible because you have no historical knowledge, his lover replies, I'll take a look at Rooms 11a to 25a then go to Room 7b, and sinks her teeth into his gums and walks away. The poet scribbles down: You won't be able to keep from returning. You'll get lost for sure. Suddenly his lover turns on the light in Room 19c and enters the room in which the portrait of his singing mother hangs: Dear Withered Child, you who have faded even before you could bloom, go far away to a world unimaginable to me and never ever return. The poet's lover says, I can even read upside down, and goes in through an entrance without a door carrying the poet's umbilical cord and points and giggles at the marble sculpture on the wooden stand, the poet's death-mask-forest. The moment the poet moves about in his sleep and predictably says that the museum's narrative is chronological, the lover thrusts into his wound her lamp-hot lips. His lover enters Room 23c through an ear then leaves through the mouth, then stops and reenters the room and knocks on the door of the poet's death, which he kneads day and night. In the basement, an exhibition: rows of portraits of the poet look like faces stuck on hemp towels. In here, when the poet puts a candle on top of his hat and looks into the mirror, he becomes absorbed in drawing himself. The poet quickly adds to his self-portrait the faint silhouette of his lover who has returned to Room 33a. He mumbles, You merely pass through the rooms, but I can go outside only if I walk past each room sequentially. And yet his lover tears off the room numbers and throws them down at the poet's feet. The candle flame flickers, maybe the wind is blowing in the dark mountain. Inside the dark room, the poet's father stops gnawing on the poet and peeks out between the black clouds. In the room of entangled time the poet stands aimlessly, unable to find the exit.

Seoul Year 2000

Subway Line Number 2 that leaves Wangsimni Station
returns in exactly 77 minutes
Thirty years ago, it took me over two hours to walk
a little over two miles from our house surrounded by bamboo
to my school next to a pond filled with lotus blossoms
and another two hours to walk back
but now it takes less than two hours to circle Seoul
I used to see a roe deer on my way to and from school
and sometimes the deer's beautiful eyes met mine
We stood still staring at each other
but when the pine trees cried *whaawhaawhaa* like nameless young warriors
the row of telephone poles along the road screamed, We're scared we're scared
and I just froze between the screams, so I was always late for school

From Wangsimni I start reading the History of the Three Kingdoms
A new state is established. King Onjo of Paekje in the 14th year of his reign
redirected the state road to reach Seoul
Time falls like rain, vanishing under the train
During the time of King Chabi of Silla in the 5th month of the 5th year of his reign,
the Japanese invaders attacked and took over Hwalgae Fortress
and captured a thousand people prisoner
The flood in the 4th month of the 8th year caused seventeen mountains to crumble
It's as if someone's pouring time into my ear
When this train arrives again at Wangsimni it'll board new passengers
While people get on and off, while the train circles Seoul, I remain seated
and keep reading
The rain stops as the train resurfaces above the Han River
The Silla, Paekje, and Koguryŏ Kingdoms that have progressed independently
for six-hundred years end
The Han River flows, carrying the dusk, and at its tributary the froth mixes
with dusk and mushrooms
The Han River gathers up the soaring froth after circling Seoul
then smears itself with blood and heads out to the West Sea to die

During breaks in today's pouring rain the stars fell from the sky of Silla and
a black dragon soared up from the well of Paekje and muddy rain fell all day long
A white dog jumped over the castle wall and a horse carried the head of
the sixteen-year-old fighter
Crossing the train tracks between Sŏngnae and Riverside Station
While King Ŭija of Paekje reigned, all the well water in Seoul
turned blood-red, so no one was able to drink it
Many small fish jumped out of the West Sea to die
but peasants couldn't eat them all
The whole world was the color of blood
As the sunset colors the train crossing the Han River red, I close my book
and return to the place I departed from
The passengers who boarded the train with me at Wangsimni are all gone
I've travelled beyond the time marked on the magnetic strip of my ticket
I'll probably get caught by the station guard at the ticket gate

History of the Three Kingdoms [Samguksagi], completed in 1145, is Korea's oldest extant
history of the Three Kingdoms—Koguryŏ, Paekje, and Silla—era of Korean history (ca. 57
BCE-935 CE).

Candy

I wake up and find
a gigantic tongue licking me
Look at the saliva dripping all over my body

The wet tongue is enormous
it licks me
Hollow teeth chew on it
From which part of its flesh did I get cut out?
I look at myself as if I am looking at a lump of flesh
Every night the bed gets soaked
Inside the wet hole, I toss and turn
Now the tongue dripping with saliva fumbles through my hair
A department store also comes and lies next to me
The tongue licks it
Cars circle the department store on the bed
flashing their lights
Even in sleep, I wear my wet glasses and stroke
the department store dripping with saliva
Transparent teeth bite my hand, bite my face
I lose my candy-sweet youth and become wrinkled with age
I hug the department store
The dripping tongue licks us both

(Mist lets
the department store slowly melt
in its mouth all night long)

The Road as a Theme for a Meal 1

For instance, the roads
can be eaten like spaghetti wrapped around a fork

but you are supposed to have it
on hot spaghetti noodles
with dark-red sauce
the way the dark-red sun gets poured
on to the hot summer shredded roads
and squirms
Look, she's stopped eating her spaghetti
folds her napkin to scribble something
It must be so hot, for her eyes are tearing
Tonight, beneath the window of a Friday where she is sitting
someone must be wrapping the red noodle-like roads
around her fork and eating them
The roads are getting pulled somewhere

Ah, when the roads get all entangled like this
have some spaghetti alone, slowly
Sit at the Friday dining table under the window high up
and wait for many centuries
Gulp down the noodles with red sauce like lava
leave only the sand plate painted red by the sauce
the way the wind peels and eats the mountain ridge
the way the sand drinks up the sea
the way she eats the distant him

I'll Call Those Things My Cats

They're alive: I'll talk about my invisible cats. They're alive. They lay two eggs every day. If they don't, they won't be able to multiply. After spring-cleaning, they're in danger of extinction. They disperse with a single puff. Yet, the cats are always alive in every corner.

They're very tiny: I don't need to give them anything to eat. Because I who am visible always leave flakes of my dead skin for them. Because my cats are tiny enough to build an apartment inside a single flake of dead skin.

They barely survive: They fall off when brushed off, they get eaten when sucked up, they put down their tails at the smallest cough. My cats are so tiny that when they are placed under a microscope and magnified 500, 1000 times you can barely see their adorable moving lips. There's one that is fairly big. It's floating in air but always at the fringes of the dust. It trembles, afraid it might get blown away when I let out my breath, even afraid to be touched by a feather. They are powerless against the cold. In summer, I can't even open the doors. They barely survive. Poor things. Please call me mother of cats. They're so tiny that I won't be able to embrace them. It can't be helped. I need to stow them in my pores at least. A red cat peeks out between the lines of a book. Such a cute thing. The cats are everywhere. They are in the center of my brain cells. Two eggs per day. Two eggs under a blanket. Red eyes, sweet cries. My cats that wiggle behind the sofa. When I return from school, they cover themselves with a blanket of dust on top of the closet—the sound of them purring, crying.

However: These adorable things. When my life gives out, they'd eat me up in a second. When it rains, they make me drag a leather sofa outdoors. They even build houses inside my nostrils. They'd even devour my elephant. They are like the stars that can't be seen in daylight.

Again, I Will Call You My Muse

Again, I will call you my muse
The life span of each muse varies, but they are always alive
Muses multiply by themselves, they even produce litters
I call out the names of my muses one by one

Empty-match-box-muse. Chocolate-wrap-muse. Already-read-newspaper-muse.
286-Computer-muse. Washer-and-dryer-combo-muse. Brand-name-Elephant-
rice-cooker-muse. There is no end to crumpling the foil-muse and calling it
affectionate names. One muse was friendly enough to come up to me wearing a
nametag, even bring its family genealogy papers. Nature-made-muse, man-made-
muse, muse that Mother packed for me when I married. Still that is not enough,
so I buy new muses daily. Sometimes, when it is too expensive, I pay by the
month. It was tiresome waiting for the muse to be delivered. Anyhow, there are
life spans to the muses. Many muses died next to me regardless of whether I gave
them a name or not. My autobiography buys new muses daily, and it can only
leave a record of how many dead muses it throws out. The big muses are filled
endlessly with little muses. Do dead muses also produce litters?

My house in which a rice-cooker-muse nurtures a maggot-muse in my absence
A muse lays a muse, lays, lays again
Must get on the forklift and barge into the house full of muses
My house that becomes a heaven of muses when the street sweeper doesn't come for ten
days
My happy house in which my muses are left to fend for themselves—they glare at the
opportunity to produce litters on the last day of the world

How about the collapsed-department-store-muse? That place became the
incarnation of muses as the walls crumbled. At least a statue of a muse-goddess
should be erected. The conversations of people crushed under the muses inside
the collapsed store. A woman whose thigh is caught between metal rods on
the 3rd floor of the basement endlessly pages her pager and calls home on her
cell phone: Hello, hello, I don't think the phone is working…. I devote my life
to washing, wiping, mending, and ironing my muses. I discard the dead ones
and take care of the live ones. I tidy them up, wash their faces, and hug them. I
wonder if, someday, I might become a muse myself, embraced by a muse.

It is written on the newspaper, back of the Chosŏn-Daily-muse, which arrived in the morning, that the entire world has declared war on the corpses of the muses. The muses will become wild when I die, the houseful of muses will fiercely multiply even after they are dead. Despite all that, this afternoon, I engraved the following on the back of a one-eyed-computer-muse:

> *When I moved, I abandoned*
> *a blue-eyed-black-cat-muse*
> *because I heard that when a muse lives*
> *with you for a long time it turns into a ghost*
> *But after three days, my family saw*
> *the black-cat-muse fly up to the window*
> *of our new house and cry all night*
> *The eyes of the cat-muse gleamed ice-blue*
> *intense enough to burn a hole through the glass*
> *Even the new-fridge-muse shook*
> *with fear all night long*

Entering the Layers of Your Text

I am reading *The Old Man Who Read Love Stories* again,
in between pages 109 and 111
The indigenous old man in the book lies in a hammock
at the entrance of the Amazon Rainforest
and fantasizes about Venice and the lovers on gondolas, and in between,
I visit Puan to see the mountains with totem poles then return
The people of the ancient times said that the land of Puan looked like a departing boat
They must have gone around reading the land as if reading a book
The boat must have had an anchor and a mast, of course, so they raised the mast
and set down the anchor
The old man in the book twirls about
unable to fantasize the gondolas, the gondolas floating about the city, and in between,
inside the jungle, a wildcat that has lost her mate to the poacher's gun
begins to attack people

The old man turns over the pages and gets stuck in the passage about
a painful kiss. How can a kiss be painful?
While he strokes the lips of his indigenous wife who died in childbirth,
the old man reads the love story and Sepulveda reads the old man and
I read Sepulveda and the invisible you read me, and in between,
I touch once again the stone totem statues covered in bumps
The husband statue opens his stone-eyes wide and looks down at his wife who has lost
her head
Unable to breathe, the sea cries and wheezes below the reclaimed land filled with
the shavings of the mountain
The mast is buried under the mudslide till only its neck shows above the slate roof
The mast that can't find its way out to the sea cries along with it
In between the pages of the book, the wildcat is still circling the snowfield with its
blood-hot eyes
The old man stops mixing up the kiss and the pain
and exits the book and roams the jungle looking for the wildcat that lost her mate,
and in between, I return to Seoul without stopping at any stations
circling the layers of your text

Poor Love Machines Trapped in Rain

The crushed body gets erased
then is crushed again
the way a painter shakes a brush
and keeps drawing thin lines
in order to keep lifting up
the body about to be crushed

Inside Café Pulp, the chairs are as narrow as bathtubs
That guy looks like he's imitating a fish
His lips pucker, blowing out rings of cigarette smoke
That guy is like a dog soaked in rain
barking alone, grabbing the phone attached to the tub
The phone is silent like a red aborted infant
I want to hide the phone under my skirt

I start a conversation with someone
I would like to have in front of me
"Please think again"
I lick that someone's wet hair
with my tongue which is like a dirty mop

The searchlight strokes our hair once
I hold up my arms
like a sleepwalker and
head towards the metal fence
made of water
Those poor love machines
are still barking
like chained dogs

Seoul's Dinner

Flowers enter. The flowers with puckered lips. The flowers that fill the back of a truck suck on the wall of the tunnel. The tunnel ripens red momentarily. She plucks off the new leaves and shoves them into her mouth. Angelica shoots drop from angelica trees and fall into the dish of seasoned soy sauce. A truckload of angelica enters. Angelica shoots turn the mouth of Seoul green. Flatfish enter. A thousand flatfish packed in ice enter, swooning. A truckload of the East Sea enters. Pigs enter. The pigs oink and suck on Seoul's lips. She dips the meat from the pig's neck in pickled shrimp and eats. Her squirming throat is omnivorous. Mudfish pour in like a muddy stream. The T'aebaek range is shredded and enters, squirming. The alpine fields of Mount Sŏrak enter, salted. Radishes revealing only the top half of their white bottoms are neatly stacked onto a truck. Trucks with their lights on enter. They line up and enter in between the teeth. When the trucks leave the tunnel, Seoul's dark-blue stomach acid covers them. Some of the trucks with big eyes try to make their way through the sea of acid, but the darkness inside Seoul's intestine is dense. Vegetables in sacks enter. Thousands of chickens with reddened crowns follow thousands of eggs just laid today and enter. Bulls as big as elephants, their eyes fiercely opened, enter. Bulls charge the road inside of someone who lives in Seoul. Tonight she drinks too much *soju*. The tunnel where the liquor is poured is long and dark. White milk that could overflow Lake Soyang pours out of the tunnel into the night's intestine. The plains of Honam enter. But in the opposite lane, trucks loaded with septic tanks have lined up in single file. Having left the party, I begin to vomit as soon as I step outside. Seoul eats and shits through the same door. My body curls up like a worm. It seems that every few days a big hand descends from the sky to roll out cloud-like toilet paper and wipe the opening of Seoul, which is simultaneously a mouth and an anus. Tonight, fat flakes fall as the last truck leaves the tunnel. I let the snow collect, then shove it into my mouth.

Wretched

On that day white paper got stamped as always *bam bam* and that day wine glasses also were filled then emptied and the women pulled down their skirts and shouted, Get your hands off of me, and that day as always he rolled down the car window and spat and the chair spun and multicolored ties flapped like flags and the 9 o'clock news showed fifty-nine men's white shirts and shoeshine boys spat on shoes to shine them

She's pregnant with the enemy soldier's baby, all she does is take naps, her belly keeps growing, her breasts get bigger and because no one has given her the stamp of approval she's not permitted to do anything, so she can't go to the supermarket to the movies to neighborhood meetings, she got her head shaved, she got dragged around the streets, she endured each day that no one came home, her eyes became big like a buffalo's because she's in her last month of pregnancy, she goes up to the 25th floor as her baby begins to come out

A buffalo jumps from the roof of the 25th floor, the Animal World's camera follows the buffalo that is chased by a lion, the buffalo giving birth to its young ends up being chased by a pack of lions, the calf that poked out its head and front legs from its mother dies from shock so the buffalo without hands unable to pull the rest of the dead calf from its womb roams the field with the front-half of the calf still hanging from it, Please pull out my dead calf, the buffalo collapses then moves about and collapses again, the field of hot sun quickly decomposes the dead calf, the herd of buffalos has crossed the river long ago, alone mommy buffalo's eyes become bigger and bigger

Possessed

Returning from playing at night with the wooden ducks
their heads stuck out between the sacred trees in Udong Village
I wondered who played with these crystal beads
Swoosh swoosh a rain shower blew in
Every crystal bead
the countless faces of those who have lived in this world then departed
their faces dripped down the car window

When I took a night bus and returned to Seoul
a woman's face wearing glasses was engraved on the black mirror
The shattered crystal beads touched
her face all over on the mirror
then rolled down
Tonight a single drop of water
circles the sky and earth and takes photos

I get off the bus and enter the whirling beads
The countless faces stretch out countless hands
I'm taken captive by the country inside the black mirror
The country where the wooden ducks are
hung high from the tips of the poles

A Blazing Buddhist Temple

Maybe it's the wind, maybe someone's calling me, so when I open the gate and look out
a Buddhist temple stands alone in flames
it's even inside the toilet bowl as I sob from diarrhea
Every time I wrap myself in my bedding and turn
the blazing temple knocks on my forehead and it's already dawn
When I get up to turn off the light the blazing temple
fills my entire room

My family has all gone out
now I can mumble as much as I want like a rain-drenched monk
The in-between time of not-night, not-day
the time when time's purplish gravy overflows
A streetlamp crosses the crosswalk
No, the streetlamp is discarded and the blazing temple attacks again
A dragon's tongue appears briefly inside the flame
It falls onto the floor, making the landscape ring
the fluttering burning robe of the head monk

As a car passes by emitting light
the ashes blow away and only the temple's pillars and cornerstones remain
Do you remember? Spending a night at the Mirŭk Temple?
We drank whisky from the cap of the bottle
and kept trying to reignite the temple in our hearts
Ah, you-u must leave and I-i must leave, we rubbed the song onto the field of reeds
In darkness a peony darker than night bloomed
The hot roof tiles suddenly vaulted up

I don't turn on the lights or make dinner
I'm pushed about by the darkness
Mumbling to myself, I open the window and watch
all the blazing temples of my lifetime
Let's scatter the beads from the burnt remains beneath our feet

A ball of flames lands at the gate of nirvana
After you die, you are reborn then die again, die then are reborn and die again
In infinite time even this skin will vanish
The scriptures carried from faraway countries, the red drapes, the sacred images
are blazing, blooming once again
They open the gate and go deep into the dark forest and never come out again

Listening to the Twelve Roars of the Spectators at Chamsil Baseball Stadium While Waiting for My Bus

1
Boom, thunder claps just once.

2
The giggling thunder. Thousands of coke bottles rolling on top of the pavement.

3
Like when thousands of tin roofs are smashed down with a single blow, but after this the river ripples, ripples, ripples…the thunder spreads, trembling.

4
A sporadic thundering, it lasts for a few minutes as if stroking a valley after a protracted silence.

5
As if the moaning, coughing, moaning, twenty thousand bundles of moaning are splitting the trees along the roadside

6
The drum as big as a baseball stadium.

7
The thunder with its fists clenched. Dump trucks swarm in a circle, dumping thousands of pebbles all at once, and twenty thousand people hold a pebble in each hand and throw them in unison into the deep water.

8
The valleys are giggling. The thunder comes partway down this valley, then that valley again, then rolls down the distant valley like a ghostly light, giggling.

9

After holding back, the clapping of thunder. Ah what a fright, the crashing sound of thunder, like a cat landing on my shoulder out of nowhere.

10

Boom! It rumbles once then in shorter and shorter claps, like the way thunder follows after a murmuring brook below the waterfall.

11

No sound, yet the sleeping babies of Chamsil Apartment wake up and cry in unison.

12

Whispering, whispering. The whispering sound rattles all the windows of Chamsil Apartment. The lightning is nowhere to be seen, the hidden thunder.

A circular staircase filled with lit faces. The searchlight moves through, buzzing each time. God startled by the laughing thunder quickly descends. He uses the faces as stepping stones, running one two three four. The spectators stand, then sit, then stand again. The monsoonal front lines keep getting etched.

In the distance the stadium glows even at night
like a blossom
and inside it a cloudbank moves about
rises high up the sky, then falls
and bursts

They've Done Taken My Blues and Gone

Someone, no, they stick straws into my body
and suck me up through the straws
The map of my body wilts
Trees fall and the wrinkles of the continents crumble
Sand hills soar

The image thieves
they steal my bones as if taking x-rays of my body
they tear away the bricks of speech whenever they can
their eyes are lit like floral oil lamps
and their snouts elongated like straws

What's a desert?
A place where a poet's empty body
stretches across the continents, manufacturing death
There is a shabby house in the desert
the curtains made of rags flutter
the sand of death crumbles and blows away

Please suck up the sand too

"They've Done Taken My Blues and Gone," a poem by Langston Hughes

To Arrive in Seoul on a Saturday Night

It's after midnight
Like the driver and two drunks blacked out
on a bus with brights on
zipping through the streets of Chongno
like the white neon sign of an emergency room
unblinking all night
like the patients, more than a thousand of them laid up on IVs
at a general hospital
like the screaming, crying phones in see-through dresses on every table
at Café Pulp
like the pagers, public phones, and ads that roam wildly
behind the shut doors of the eclipse of the brightly-lit Myŏngdong district
like the grandfather, grandmother, mommy, and younger sibling running with the
clothes they've just taken off towards "my beautiful laundrette" that remains lit 24
hours a day
When you look down from Mount South
the hour everything's asleep
the blazing golden rose in the middle of Seoul
This bright heaven
like the South Gate Market!

Someone
walks by swishing
like a dollar fishbowl

Conservatism of the Rats of Seoul

Daddy and Mommy lay us down one by one
Many of us are born—as many as Mommy's nipples
Mommy licks our eyes with her tongue softer than white bread,
licks with all her might, with darkness, darkness is cozy

Daddy who herds a fish head home also brings with him scary news
You can hear the footsteps far away, the wailing fire truck
Mommy's nipples harden
Mommy blocks the rat hole with her entire body,
our ears as well

A hairy leg enters our room. It's him. He thrashes his body around,
bam bam, shaking the house, but only the leg enters,
toenails rip Mommy's eyes, ears,
the foot in a leather shoe stomps on Mommy's skirt
Mommy isn't breathing

He pokes around, back and forth
as many times as the minute hand of the night
You can hear the snarl all night long
He wails, pounding his head against the wall
Mommy is like a corpse and Daddy is nowhere to be seen
All night long, crushed against the house,
a hairy mouth tries to get in

By morning all is quiet--he must have left
Mommy finally gets up and breathes
Mommy bites and kills each one of us
for giving off a suspicious scent from last night's terror
She kills us then eats our intestines,
grinds her teeth against a wall
then digs out our eyeballs to eat
then there is no one
As always, only Daddy and Mommy are left
It looks as if Mommy is expecting another litter

The Rat Race

Wherever I meet you, you are always on the run
from Scorpio to Libra
from Libra to Taurus
Not here, not here
From the potato sack to the rice sack
from the soap dish to the bottom of the desk
from Lukács to Deleuze
from the basement to the attic
from the septic tank to the cemetery
I hate all things that are shiny and black
You are always on the run
from the deep to the surface

Where are you really?
Am I the dream you dreamt inside my body?
Am I the dream you pulled up with chopsticks from the 39-degree-Celsius fever?
Did we meet as we gnawed on a corpse and rolled around inside the grave?
Where, where was that place?
Not here, not here
This is the inside of somebody's skull—
you can't look out without the two black holes

You say you will move from the age of Pisces to Aquarius
You pack every day, saying someday you will leave Seoul
Yet, tonight, in Seoul, where I am chased as if by a cat
we spill out from the underground Tongdaemun rail station
get sucked up into somebody's flute

like a pack of rats

Silent Night, Holy Night

It was already too late when I dug into the grave, the corpse that had already been devoured by rats showed up and my back ached. The organs inside my back ached, the organs shrieked and rattled my ribs and a hired man said that if I wanted to find a fat rat I needed to turn this cemetery inside out. It was fashionable to have babies in your forties and, strangely, azaleas blossomed from a rose bush and acacias smelled like lilacs. Pyŏkje Cremation was busy nonstop and mismatched legs kept arriving and piling into the coffin and in one coffin there was only the hand of a woman. The mortician was dead on her feet. I flew to Spain to watch flamenco and watched it again as I rotated once, for 12 beats, rotated twice, for 24, and repeated, O Time, be gone, be gone, and from where I was sitting I wished for many lifetimes to pass. My lover would only talk to me in code and a Japanese critic was up in arms, That's just how I am. What's your story? Even though I was told that scorpions were submerged inside the rain-soaked mud, I dug it up and smeared it on my face. The president of each country signed an exchange so that the corpses of dead husbands could be returned as Christmas gifts from the war-torn country and my students shouted towards the screen Nature! But my fellow poets ripped the screen and shouted towards the darkness, Here is nature, and we carefully considered whether the remaining enemy of Father was also our enemy. While we were deep in thought, only the female factory workers who weren't hooked up to the internet bought fiction. Then one day, I raise the lid of the manhole that empties into the canal. The rats that open their eyes only in the dark, their eyes that have turned the color of sewage, their teeth that have become sharp as picks from digging around with their black eyes open. The rats startled by the light trickling in run away with their hairless litters that have just opened their eyes in their mother's embrace and

A Way to Read the Morning

In January, many stars fell like rain, but they fell only into the river, unable to reach the land.

In February, the scripture that I read daily packed up its bag and took off to another country like the missing child of the universe, like floating fish, like the Space Shuttle Challenger. (Bad guy!)

In March, all the fish came out of the frozen river and died.

In April, the scales of the stars that fell nonstop piled up. The north was still ferocious.

In May, obstructions were everywhere, TV screens were always on, the river empty of fish flowed by.

In June, the department store south of Han River sank into the ground, becoming a crater, and those who saw apples in their dreams made it out alive.

In July, the underground wells overflowed, causing the houses to float away, and the pigs cried on top of the roofs. Instead of the trains, the crimson river whistled and streamed down the tracks.

In August, a reddish cloud from the southeast rolled out like silk, then it rained, and the fish fell too mixed in with the rain.

In September, the wind came to the front of the door and cried, Open up, open up. Next morning, a bundle of the wind's hair was found tangled around the doorknob. It was the full moon. A place other than east west south north was most auspicious. Did he also shoot all six bullets?

In October, cherry blossoms suddenly bloomed in late autumn. I kept thinking about him every time they bloomed. Dead fish floated up all white along the riverbank.

At eleventh moon...

At twelfth moon, with thirty seconds left to dream, the river froze again. White out. Every time I took a wrong step, I fell into the thousands of roads, below the crevasses, into the river's blue teeth. The blanket is white like the South Pole and an iceberg floated beneath it. He soldered me to the same circuit again.

Again in January,

Translator's Note

we howl and we shriek and we translate – Daniel Borzutzky[i]

Double p—How Creepy – Kim Hyesoon[ii]

Kim Hyesoon's *Poor Love Machine* [*Pulssanghan sarang kigye*] was published in Seoul, in 1997, and was chosen for the coveted Kim Su-yŏng Poetry Prize. Kim Su-yŏng (1921-1968) was a major poet, who is associated with "engaged poetry" [*ch'amyŏsi*]—one of the two trends that dominated modern Korean poetry since the early 20th century—poetry that displays social, historical awareness as opposed to "pure poetry" [sunsusi], which stood for art for art sake. When, in 1997, Kim Hyesoon became the first female poet to receive the prestigious award, she thought that this ground-breaking, critical recognition was due to the emergence of women's poetry during the 1980s (when Kim also emerged) through the 90's, at which point the male-dominated South Korean literary establishment could no longer ignore it. Kim has noted that "the father of women poets during the 1980s was a father who enforced a triple form of oppression on women: a father who oppressed an individual socially and politically, who crushed gender equality, and who mandated that women form their identity from the margins."[iii] Therefore, within the context of South Korea, the recognition of *Poor Love Machine* signaled a major breakthrough and shift in the status of women's poetry.

The 1990's also marks an important shift in South Korea's history. After the three decades of oppressive military dictatorship, not to mention the devastating Korean War (1950-53), which claimed nearly four million lives as well as the three decades of brutal Japanese colonial rule that preceded the war, South Korea finally entered the era of civilian rule in 1993 with the election of the first civilian president. A peace and justice activist and historian, George Katsiaficas points out that the democratization of South Korea, its transition to civilian rule, was not elite-led or top-down as it has been portrayed by certain think tanks in the U.S. The civil society came to be realized through many sacrifices: from the 1960 Student Uprising, the 1980 Gwangju Uprising, the *minjung* [people] democratic movement that involved countless student and labor protests, to the June Uprising of 1987, when even office workers and ordinary citizens joined massive demonstrations in downtown Seoul, demanding basic human rights, direct elections, freedom of the press, reunification of the two Koreas, release of political prisoners, and the end of dictatorship.[iv]

Katsiaficas makes a critical connection between dictatorships and neoliberalism:

> Before the consolidation of neoliberal accumulation regimes in Chile and Korea, the United States needed strong dictatorships to suppress strong insurgent movements that sought indigenous control of local resources and markets. Once this process had occurred and billions of U.S. dollars in corporate investments had been made, the possibility of the emergence of a radical movement that might overthrow the accumulation regime was actually made more likely by dictatorships. Once best friends of the United States, military rulers became threats to economic investments of U.S. corporations and banks, and a transition to a new type of accumulation regime was required to safeguard the investments lucratively made under the military dictatorships. In 1987, fearing a nationwide insurrection against Chun [Doo-hwan] could result in a radical shift in Korea, the United States moved on without him."[v]

For Chile, it was 1988, when the United States moved on without Pinochet. Thank you, Chicago Boys. We thank you. In fact, South Korea's very first free trade agreement with another country was with Chile, which has been in effect for twelve years now. What is at stake are not merely cheap grapes, bacon, cars, and smartphones, but the degradation of the lives and lands of indigenous communities and farmers on both sides of the equator. The Korea-US Free Trade Agreement that went into effect in 2012 was a reinforcement of the neoliberal agenda. And the pending trade agreement, the Trans-Pacific Partnership (TPP), adds one more boost, which is to say, it is an apparatus of imperialism that will further enrich multinational corporations and banks, including the expansion of U.S. military in the Asia-Pacific Region. Hence, the construction of a new U.S. Naval base on the pristine part of Jeju Island of South Korea, a UNESCO Biosphere Conservation Area, and a new state-of-the-art U.S. Marine base at Henoko, also an unspoiled ecosphere of Okinawa, Japan. The current best friends of the United States are paying for the new bases, which is to say, it is neocolonialism at its best. It not only hijacks people's lands and livelihoods, it also colonizes language. One of the warships that has recently moved into the Jeju Naval Base is an Aegis cruiser. The word Aegis comes from Greek mythology, and refers to the shield worn by Zeus and Athena. The Aegis Combat System, produced by Lockeed Martin, is a high-tech weapon control system that searches, tracks, and destroys enemy targets. I repeat: neocolonialism searches, tracks, and destroys. It does not want us to translate. Aegis Go Home! Without shields, *we howl and we shriek and we translate*

> Translation (T) is against the neoliberal Trans
> (T) is against the neocolonial Trans
> (T) will never be your best friend
> (T)PP
> Go on, p and p
> *Double p–How creepy*

And we remember

> Aimé Césaire: colonization = "thingification"[vi]

South Korean women played an important role in the populist *minjung* movement by leading independent union activities, banned during the dictatorship. Korean feminism of the 1970s and 80s is rooted in the earlier Korean socialist feminism of the 1930s, during Korea's colonial period, which made links between class, gender, and nation as a challenge to women's oppression. One of the important feminist organizations to emerge during the 1980's was Another Culture [*ttohana ŭi munhwa*], and Kim Hyesoon was an active member of the organization and contributed to the publication of feminist literature and criticism. At a gathering of writers and scholars, four months prior to the June Uprising of 1987, Korean feminist literature was explored in the context of the women's movement, and was understood as a "literature of indictment," and a part of *minjung* literature. Kim says that during the 1980s literary critics have demanded that she "enter the sea of society," meaning her poetry was not considered to be engaged in social resistance. She says her poetry did not appear to be political because "what I wrote about was cooking and my ingredient was death."[vii] In her poem "Heavenly Ramen," humans, mushrooms, delusions make up the ingredients in the soup of death:

Like when the sky boils a star for a long time
60 million humans, countless mushrooms
and even more countless fish come out
When you boil the earth's night, the night's delusions
for a long time
(I lift the lid and
watch my boiling brain)

And in her interview with Ruth Williams, Kim says that she "came to grotesque language in the patriarchal culture under the dictatorship… So the miserable images I use in my poems are the same as the letters I send into the miserable world."[viii] Kim offers us many memorable images in *Poor Love Machine*: the images of corpses and rats with eyes that have turned the color of sewage in "Silent Night, Holy Night"; a rat devouring a rabbit, a piglet, a newborn in "This Night"; a mommy rat and her hard nipples in "Conservatism of the Rats of Seoul"; a dead calf dangling from mommy buffalo in "Wretched." Under the miserable dictatorship, we are "chunks of freshly grilled flesh inside a womb," we are "the bloody foam of the flowering field," we are "the [Sampoong] department store dripping with saliva," which collapsed in 1995, killing 502 people—a neoliberal-terror-related building collapse, we are the "mismatched legs [that] kept arriving and piling into the coffin," we are "red eyes, sweet cries," we "barely survive." "Poor things"—we are "poor love machines":

The searchlight strokes our hair once
I hold up my arms
like a sleepwalker and
head towards the metal fence
made of water
Those poor love machines
are still barking
like chained dogs

Elfriede Jelinek observes the twoness of translation: "I translate myself, so I know what it means: one follows someone's text which one actually wrote oneself before."[ix] I howl and I shriek and I translate. So the miserable images I translate are the same as the letters I send into the miserable world. I come to translation, the language of echoing, the language of howling, under the U.S. imperialism. Translation = Antithingification

In 2012, Kim Hyesoon was one of the 250 poets who participated in the largest poetry festival in the U.K. When SJ Fowler asked Kim how she felt about being a representative of her nation for Poetry Parnassus, she answered, "I am a poet from the nation called, The Poet, Kim Hyesoon."[x] Under patriarchy, under dictatorship, under neocolonialism, Kim has been engaged in nation-building of her own, which she calls "My Republic of Poetry"[xi]:

> I hope that my poetry has the same structure as a mandala. The kind of structure that binds the inside and the outside together. Also, I hope my poetry attains the method of reading the world with my body embedded in it like the way a fractal form does.
>
> Inside her own body, a woman rises and fades and observes the identity of her death and life like the waxing and waning moon. Therefore, a woman's body is an infinite fractal. Through the method of reading the fractal, I live as a woman, feeling and following the road through which life flows in and out. I love therefore I become myself. I love, so my body can draw a mandala as beautiful as the moon's cycle.
>
> This love has flowed out from my female body for eons and the distinct voice of my existence has burst out from that place. But the essence of this existence is not a fixed form but a moving essence. Its cycle never ends. But it never draws the same form.

My cycle of translation has never ceased since my first encounter with Kim's poetry in 1998. Under Kim Hyesoon's republic of poetry, I howl and I shriek and I translate.

Kim mentioned to me several years ago that *Seoul, My Upanishad*, published three years before *Poor Love Machine*, felt to her as if she was finally figuring out the way she wanted to write. In a more recent interview, Kim says that "the ignition point for poetry is multiple, but the material for ignition is one. My body has to be in a poetic state."[xii] In *Poor Love Machine*, Kim Hyesoon's grotesque language is in full bloom, becoming an ignition point for her subsequent books, *All the Garbage of the World, Unite!* and *Sorrowtoothpaste Mirrocream*, in which her grotesque language plays out magnificently in poems such as "Manhole Humanity" and "I'm Ok, I'm Pig!" The miserable images of the rats, pigs, holes, garbage, and other ingredients of death make up the body—the body of Kim's poetry. *Poor Love Machine* is Kim Hyesoon's poetic state.

> Seoul eats and shits through the same door. My body curls up like
> a worm. It seems that every few days a big hand descends from the
> sky to roll out cloud-like toilet paper and wipe the opening of Seoul,
> which is simultaneously a mouth and an anus.

Poor Love Machine is simultaneously the mouth and anus of Kim Hyesoon's republic of poetry.

Kim's republic of poetry is also the ignition point for younger Korean women poets who are "developing a terrain of poetry that is combative, visceral, subversive, inventive, and ontologically feminine."[xiii]

Don Mee Choi
Seattle, Jan 23, 2016

[i]Daniel Borzutzky, *Memories of My Overdevelopment* (Chicago: Kenning Editions, 2015), 18.

[ii]Kim Hyesoon, *All the Garbage of the World, Unite!*, trans. Don Mee Choi (Notre Dame: Action Books, 2011), 67.

[iii]Ch'oe Sŭng-ja, Kim Hyesoon, and Yi Yŏn-ju, *Anxiety of Words: Contemporary Poetry by Korean Women*, trans. Don Mee Choi (Brookline: Zephyr, 2006), xviii-xix.

[iv]George Katsiaficas, *Asia's Unknown Uprisings: South Korean Social Movements in the 20th Century* (Oakland: PM, 2012), 244-298.

[v]Ibid., 300-305,

[vi]Aimé Césaire, *Discourse on Colonialism*, trans. Joan Pinkham (New York: Monthly Review Press, 2000), 42.

[vii]Ch'oe, Kim, Yi, *Anxiety*, xvii-xviii.

[viii]Ruth Williams, "The Female Grotesque: Ruth Williams Interviews Kim Hyesoon," *Guernica*, Jan 1, 2012.

[ix]Elfriede Jelinek, *Rechnitz and The Merchant's Contracts*, trans. and intro. Gitta Honegger (London, New York, Calcutta: Seagull Books, 2015), 1.

[x]"SJ Fowler Interviews Kim Hyesoon for the Poetry Parnassus," accessed January 22, 2016, http://www.southbankcentre.co/uk/poetry-parnassus/poets/hyesoon-kim.

[xi]Kim Hyesoon, *Yŏsŏngi kŭrŭl ssŭndanŭn kŏsŭn* (Seoul: Munhakdongne, 2002), 227-233.

[xii]Kim Hyesoon, *Sorrowtoothpaste Mirrorcream*, trans. Don Mee Choi (Notre Dame: Action Books, 2014), 96.

[xiii]Kim, *Sorrowtoothpaste Mirrorcream*, 94.

Acknowledgements:

The translation of *Poor Love Machine* was supported by a generous grant from the Literature Translation Institute of Korea.

Thank you to the editors of the journals in which some of the poems have appeared: *Asia Literary Review, Fairy Take Review, Feminist Studies, Modern Poetry in Translation, Paragraphiti,* and *Poetry International Web.*

My deep gratitude to Action Books for its continuous commitment to Kim Hyesoon's poetry. To Deborah Woodard and Johannes Göransson for their careful reading and suggestions. To past and present Action Books interns for their amazing work. And to Andrew Shuta for his exceptional book design.

All the poems in *Poor Love Machine* are from *Pulssanghan sarang kigye*, (Seoul: Munhak kwa chisŏng sa, 1997)

Kim, Hyesoon is one of the most prominent contemporary poets of South Korea. She lives in Seoul and teaches creative writing at the Seoul Institute of the Arts. Kim's poetry and prose in translation can be found in *When the Plug Gets Unplugged* (Tinfish, 2005), *Anxiety of Words* (Zephyr, 2006), and *Mommy Must Be a Fountain of Feathers* (Action Books, 2008), *All the Garbage of the World, Unite!* (Action Books, 2011), *Princess Abandoned* (Tinfish, 2012), *Sorrowtoothpaste Mirrorcream* (Action Books, 2014), *I'm Ok, I'm Pig!* (Bloodaxe Books, 2014), and *Trilingual Renshi* (Vagabond, 2015).

Choi, Don Mee is the author of *The Morning News is Exciting* (Action Books, 2010) and *Hardly War* (Wave Books, 2016). She has received a Whiting Award and Lucien Stryk Asian Translation Prize.